TWINKLE'S LITE

BY
Erin Gonzalez

ILLUSTRATED BY
VALENTINA DI FABIO

TWINKLE'S LITE SHINED BRIGHT IN THE DARK NIGHT SKY.

There were many stars that shared the dark night sky with Twinkle, but no one shined as brightly as she did.

Her happy mood kept her shining bright, and her kindness and love for others gave her such a glow.

THE STARS AROUND HER WOULD OFTEN TELL TWINKLE HOW BEAU-
TIFUL SHE WAS AND HOW HER LITE WAS LIKE NO OTHER..

TWINKLE WOULD RESPOND TO THE OTHERS WITH, "YOU ARE ALL
BEAUTIFUL AND ALSO HAVE A LITE LIKE NO OTHER. "WE ALL SHINE
DIFFERENTLY AND ARE BEAUTIFUL IN OUR VERY OWN WAY.

TWINKLE MEANT WHAT SHE SAID TO THE OTHER STARS WITH LOVE IN HER HEART, BUT A FEW OF THE SURROUNDING STARS DID NOT MEAN WHAT THEY SAID TO TWINKLE.

GLIMMER AND SPARKLE, WHO SHINED DIRECTLY BEHIND TWINKLE
DID NOT LIKE HOW TWINKLE SHINED.

THEY WOULD OFTEN WHISPER TO EACH OTHER AND SAY HOW
TWINKLE'S SHINE WAS TOO BRIGHT AND UNNECESSARY.

One day, Glimmer and Sparkle were whispering to each other when Twinkle heard them. Glimmer said, "Twinkle is such a show off and only wants the world to notice her!" Sparkle then said,

"There are so many of us here to brighten the night sky, but Twinkle only cares about herself!"

Twinkle couldn't believe that Glimmer and Sparkle felt this way about her. This made Twinkle very sad. Twinkle thought to herself,

"I was just being myself, and shining bright is something I love to do."

Glimmer and Sparkle's words floated in Twinkle's head so much that it started to make her spin in circles.

TWINKLE.DID NOT LIKE THIS SPINNING FEELING. SHE MADE IT
STOP BY REMEMBERING THE REASON SHE SHINES SO BRIGHTLY.

TWINKLE REMEMBERED THAT SHE LIKED BRINGING JOY AND BEAUTY TO THE WORLD AROUND HER. SHE DOES THIS BY BEING KIND AND LOVING TO ALL. TWINKLE KNEW WHAT SHE HAD TO DO NEXT.

TWINKLE WAS GOING TO KEEP ON SHINING BRIGHT
AND NOT LET OTHERS' HURTFUL WORDS CHANGE THAT.
TWINKLE DECIDED THAT SHE WAS GOING TO SHARE
HER LITE.

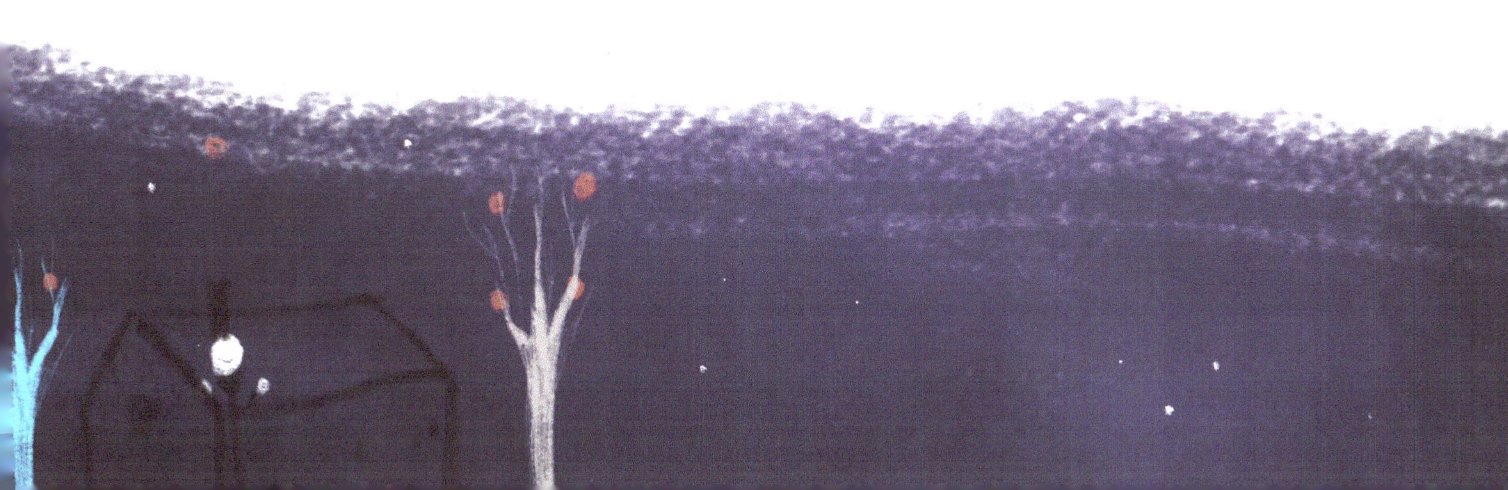

TWINKLE THOUGHT THAT IF SHE COULD SHARE SOME OF HER LITE WITH GLIMMER AND SPARKLE, THEY MIGHT FEEL THE SAME HAPPINESS SHE FEELS INSIDE. THEY COULD ALL SHINE BRIGHT TOGETHER.

THE FOLLOWING NIGHT, TWINKLE ASKED GLIMMER AND SPARKLE
IF THEY COULD GIVE HER SOME COMPANY BY STANDING WITH HER.

GLIMMER AND SPARKLE LOOKED AT EACH OTHER, A BIT CONFUSED,
AS THEY WENT OVER TO STAND BY TWINKLE'S SIDE.

Twinkle brought them in closer to her and said, "I thought we could all shine together tonight."

GLIMMER AND SPARKLE COULD FEEL TWINKLE'S LITE INSIDE OF
THEM. IT WAS A WARM AND HAPPY GLOW.

This changed the way they felt about Twinkle. It made them understand why Twinkle shined so brightly.

THE THREE STARS SHINED EVER SO BRIGHT THAT NIGHT, AND TO-
GETHER, THEY BROUGHT JOY TO THOSE LOOKING UP AT THE NIGHT
SKY.

The End.